Echoes of the Heart: A Queer Poetry Odyssey

by

Adriano Alamia

Foreword

In the pages that follow, you are invited on a profound journey into the heart of queer existence—a voyage through the intricacies of love, the depths of self-discovery, and the luminous path toward self-acceptance. This collection of poetry, a mosaic of emotions and experiences, serves not just as a window into the souls of those who walk the often-winding path of queer identity, but as a mirror reflecting the universal quest for connection, understanding, and unconditional love.

These poems, each a beacon of light in the vastness of human experience, weave together the threads of joy and sorrow, hope and despair, isolation and community, into a tapestry rich with the colors of life itself. They speak a language of courage, resilience, and the unyielding power of the human spirit to find its way out of the darkness and into the brilliance of the light.

Crafted with exquisite care and profound empathy, the verses you are about to read transcend the boundaries of identity, reaching into the core of what it means to be human. They remind us that while our journeys may differ, the desire to be seen, understood, and loved for who we truly are is universal. In the rhythm of these words, in the space between each line, there is an invitation to embrace the full spectrum of our beings, to celebrate the diversity that enriches our shared humanity.

As you turn these pages, may you find solace in knowing you are not alone in your journey. May the bravery of coming out of the shadows inspire you to live your truth with boldness and beauty. May the stories of love have found, lost, and reclaimed fill you with hope. And may the act of loving oneself, in all its forms, resonate with you, echoing through the corridors of your own heart.

This book is more than a collection of poetry; it is a declaration of pride, a chorus of voices united in the affirmation that love, in all its forms, is the most profound and powerful force we possess. It is a call to each of us, regardless of how we identify or whom we love, to stand together in the light, to support one another with compassion, and to move forward with the kind of love that transcends all barriers.

Welcome to a celebration of the heart, a journey of transformation, and a testament to the indomitable spirit of love that defines the queer experience. Welcome to the odyssey of the self, where every poem is a step towards the luminous truth that resides within us all.

Table of Contents

Out of the Shadows

In the quiet before dawn,
I walked alone,
Shadows lingering, in the dark,
I now have grown.
A whispering heart,
secrets buried deep,
Veiled in the night,
a soul in silent weep.

Through the thicket,
a faint light I spied,
A beacon of hope,
where my fears could hide.
Step by step,
towards the warmth I moved,
Each stride away from the dark,
it has proved.

In the light, my truth
began to blend,
A spectrum of colors,

no longer pretend.
I embraced the hues,
my essence, my spark,
Emerging from shadows,
into the light, stark.
Self-love, a journey,
through turmoil and strife,
Finding my worth,
in the canvas of life.
A gay man standing,
proud and unbound,
In my truth, finally,
peace I found.

Unveiling the Heart

Beneath a mask,
I hid my face,
A character played,
out of place.
In the mirror,
a stranger's gaze,
Lost in a labyrinth,
a soul's maze.

The world outside,
so vast, so bright,
Yet, I dwelled
in perpetual night.
Yearning for daylight,
for my heart's key,
To unlock the chains,
to set me free.

The moment came,
a crack in the sky,
A sliver of sun,

a sigh--a cry.
I stepped through the door,
out of the gloom,
Into a garden,
where my true self could bloom.
From darkness to light,
a path I carved,
Accepting the love,
for long starved.
A gay man's journey,
from fear to grace,
In the world's vast garden,
I found my place.

Rivers of Light

Once, I was a river,
dark and deep,
Flowing silently,
in shadows steep.
Hiding beneath the surface,
my true essence,
A current of fear,
of suppressed presence.

But rivers, they twist,
they turn--they fight,
Seeking the sea,
the source of all light.
So, I surged forward,
through the dark I dove,
Towards the ocean
of self-acceptance and love.

Breaking free
from the banks of despair,
I flowed into realms

of fresh air.
A gay man's soul,
once veiled in night,
Now glimmers brightly,
in love's pure light.
Each drop
a testament to the fight,
From the depths of darkness,
into the light.
A journey of courage,
a heart laid bare,
In the waters of love,
I found my share.

Dawn of Me

In shadows long,
I softly tread,
A silent song,
by fear led.
Hidden depths,
a quiet plea,
In twilight's grasp,
I longed to be free.

The dawn crept in,
a hesitant glow,
Illuminating paths,
feelings in tow.
A heart once cloaked
in the night's embrace,
Now basking in the light,
a newfound grace.

A gay man's journey,
from dusk till dawn,
A self-reborn,

a veil withdrawn.
In the morning light,
pure and clear,
I found my truth;
I hold it dear.

Echoes of Authenticity

Echoes in the void,
a whispering truth,
A labyrinth of youth,
a quest uncouth.
In every echo,
a part of me,
Yearning for light,
yearning to be free.

The walls resonated
with my silent cries,
Each echo, a mask,
a clever disguise.
Until one echoed louder,
clearer, and bright,
A call to arms,
for my own fight.

Through the echoes,
a path was forged,
Towards authenticity,

my essence gorged.
A gay man's echo,
no longer faint,
Painting my world
without restraint.

The Phoenix's Flight

From ashes dark,
a phoenix rose,
Above whispered fears
and shadowed foes.
Flames of truth
in his heart did burn,
A tale of resurrection,
at every turn.

His flight, a path
through night to day,
A vibrant spectrum,
not just gray.
A gay man's soul,
reborn in fire,
Rising above,
soaring higher.

In the flames,
he found his might,
From despair's depths,

into the light.
A phoenix's journey,
fierce and bright,
In love and truth,
he found his flight.

Bridge of Light

A bridge of light,
from heart to heart,
A chasm wide,
yet worlds apart.
Stepping stones,
once submerged in night,
Now illuminated,
shining bright.

Across this bridge,
I dared to tread,
With every step,
old fears shed.
A gay man's stride,
towards the sun,
A journey of love,
finally begun.

This bridge,
a symbol, sturdy and true,
Of a path to self-love,

and acceptance too.
From darkness to light,
a journey made,
On foundations of courage,
love laid.

Canvas of Me

A canvas blank,
in darkness lay,
Awaiting dawn's
first gentle ray.
Each stroke of light,
a color bold,
The story of a gay man,
remained untold.

With each hue,
I painted my soul,
Filling the void,
making me whole.
A masterpiece hidden,
now in sight,
Colors of the rainbow,
shining bright.

From shadows
to a vibrant scene,
A journey of love,

in between.
This canvas of life,
uniquely me,
In colors of love,
I found the key.

From Despair's Edge to Dawn's Embrace

In the quiet before the storm,
where whispers drown the light,
I stood alone,
at the edge of night.
A queer heart,
heavy with unseen tears,
Carrying the weight
of unspoken fears.

The world felt cold,
unforgiving, and vast,
Each day a shadow,
each breath my last.
Thoughts of surrender
to the silent call,
Where darkness promised
to cradle my fall.

Yet, in that abyss,
where hope seemed lost,

A flicker of light,
despite the frost.
A whisper softer
than despair's harsh scream,
A glimmer of something,
a distant dream.
It spoke of love,
not yet embraced,
Of days filled with light,
not erased.
A promise that dawn
comes after the night,
A battle within me,
yet to fight.

I found a spark,
hidden deep within,
A strength to rise,
a desire to begin.
To face my darkness,
my fears, my pain,
To find my rainbow
after the rain.

Step by cautious step,
I chose to climb,
Away from the edge,
leaving darkness behind.
I learned to whisper to myself,
love's gentle sound,
In my own embrace,
acceptance I found.

The journey was long,
through nights dark and deep,
But I found my light,
a promise to keep.
A queer soul,
once lost, now fiercely alive,
Embraced by the dawn,
destined to thrive.

In the mirror now,
a reflection true,
A person of worth,
through and through.
No longer a prisoner

of my own night,
I stand in my truth,
my heart alight.

Whisper of Hope

In shadow's depth,
I found my place,
A realm of silence,
void of grace.

A queer soul
adrift in endless night,
Contemplating the void,
devoid of light.

Yet, amidst despair,
a whisper faint,
A melody soft,
a painter's paint.

A thread of hope
in darkness spun,
Hinting that the night
was not yet done.

With every note,
a spark took flight,
Illuminating corners,
banishing night.

I learned to listen,
to hear--to see,
In whispers of hope,
I found the key.

From the brink I stepped,
into dawn's embrace,
A journey of healing,
a newfound grace.

A queer heart once lost,
now firmly found,
In the symphony of life,
I am profound.

The Light Within

In my deepest despair,
where light dared not tread,
I danced with thoughts,
a fragile thread.
A queer spirit,
wrestling with shadows vast,
Yearning for a future,
free from the past.

Then, in the silence,
a spark unseen,
A light within,
where darkness had been.
A force unyielding,
a fire bright,
Guiding me gently,
from night to light.

With each step forward,
the shadows receded,
My inner light,

all I ever needed.
A journey from the edge,
back to the start,
Where I learned to love,
my own queer heart.

Dawn's First Light

At night's darkest hour,
I stood alone,
A queer life,
its beauty yet to be shown.
The abyss beckoned,
a siren's call,
Promising peace,
an end to it all.

Yet, as I teetered,
on despair's edge,
I glimpsed a light,
a solemn pledge.
Dawn's first light,
breaking through despair,
Offering hope,
fresh air to breathe, to share.

Step back I did,
from the precipice,
Embracing life,

its complex tess.
A queer being,
bathed in morning's glow,
Ready to live,
to love--to grow.

Bridge Over Troubled Water

I walked a path,
so narrow, so fraught,
A queer soul,
with turmoil wrought.
The chasm of despair,
wide and deep,
Called to me,
in my weakest, to leap.

But then I saw,
amidst the strife,
A bridge of colors,
leading to life.
Each step a testament
to battles fought,
A rainbow path,
with lessons taught.

Across this bridge,
from dark to light,
I found my way,

through day and night.
A queer journey,
from fear to self-love,
Guided by hope,
from the stars above.

From Shadows to Sunlight

Cloaked in the night,
where fears converge,
A queer heart,
on the verge.
Thoughts swirling,
a tumultuous sea,
Wondering what it means
to be free.

But then, a break
in the endless gloom,
A sliver of sunlight,
dispelling doom.
It whispered of places
where love is right,
Where being oneself
isn't a fight.

So, from the shadows,
I took a step,
Into the sunlight,

a new adept.
A queer soul,
embracing the day,
Loving myself,
come what may.

Becoming

I wandered long
in twilight's embrace,
A soul in search,
a hidden face.
In every shadow,
a piece of me,
A puzzle waiting
to be free.

Self-discovery,
a journey long,
In every right,
in every wrong.
A queer heart finding
its true beat,
In every victory,
every defeat.

Self-love,
a beacon in the night,
Guiding me with

its gentle light.
I learned to embrace
all that I am,
A glorious, intricate,
beautiful jam.

The Mirror's Truth

In the mirror,
a stranger's eyes,
A facade built
on society's lies.

But deep within,
a spark remained,
A truth untouched,
Unchained--unstained.

A journey inward,
to depths unknown,
Where seeds of self-love
are immediately sown.

A queer soul,
in reflection found,
A love that's deep,
Profound--unbound.

My Own Symphony

I lived in silence,
a song unsung,
A heart unspoken,
a bell unrung.

But within me
played a melody,
A symphony of what
it means to be free.

Self-discovery,
my composition,
A life of truth,
my mission.

A queer anthem,
loud and clear,
In my own symphony,
I hold dear.

Unwritten Pages

I am a book,
pages blank and wide,
A story of love,
From the inside.

Each chapter
a step--a discovery new,
Of all the wonders
that make me, me and you, you.

Self-love penned
in every line,
A queer tale,
both yours and mine.

Coming to terms
with who we are,
Shining bright—
a guiding star.

Colors of Me

In a world
of black and white,
I found my colors,
bright and light.

Reds and yellows,
greens and blues,
A spectrum of me,
a rainbow of hues.

Self-discovery
in every shade,
A canvas of love,
personally made.

A queer life,
vibrant and true,
Embracing myself,
through and through.

Echoes of Me

Echoes of a life
once hidden,
Whispers of dreams,
once forbidden.

In the echoes,
I found my voice,
A queer soul,
making a choice.

Self-love in every echo—
every sound,
In my truth,
I am found.

Coming to terms,
with open arms,
Cherishing every
one of my charms.

From Shadows to Stars

From the shadows,
I stepped into light,
From the depths,
I took flight.

A journey of self,
through the night,
Towards the stars,
Oh--so bright.

Self-discovery,
a path to the skies,
A queer spirit,
wise and wise.

Loving myself,
in the vast expanse,
In the universe,
I dance.

Reflections in the Water

In still waters,
I saw my face,
A reflection of grace—
of space.

In the ripples,
a story told,
Of a queer soul,
bold and bold.

Self-discovery
in every wave,
A journey of love,
brave and brave.

Coming to terms
with my reflection,
In every ripple—
a new direction.

The Road Less Traveled

On the road less traveled,
I found my way,
Through forests--dense,
through night and day.

A path of self,
winding and long,
A queer journey,
where I belong.

Self-love on this road--
my guide,
With every step,
a widening stride.

Coming to terms
with the path I choose,
In every footprint—
I infuse.

Rising Dawn

In the quiet of the dawn--
I rise,
A soul awakened—
wise and wise.

From darkness to light—
a transformation,
A queer being—
a new creation.

Self-discovery
in the morning glow,
A journey of love,
to know and know.

Coming to terms
with the light of day,
In love with myself—
in every way.

Whispered Winds Extended

In whispered winds,
our secret lies,
A tale of love,
under watchful skies.
A note to you,
from depths profound,
Where words of love,
in silence, are found.

In every breeze
that brushes your skin,
Feel my love—
from within.
A clandestine dance
of shadows and light,
Our love--a phoenix,
taking flight.

Though the world may not see,
nor understand,
Our hearts beat together,

hand in hand.
In whispered winds,
our vows we exchange,
A love so deep,
it will never change.

Shadows' Embrace Extended

In shadows' embrace,
we steal our moments,
A love so fierce,
yet tender its components.
A secret note,
from my heart to yours,
In a world that judges,
our love endures.

Beneath the moon's silent,
watchful eye,
Our love takes wing,
in the night sky.
Hidden from view,
but felt so deep,
In the shadows' embrace,
our promises we keep.

Let the night be our witness,
the stars our scribe,
Recording our love—

the only vibe.
In this secret place,
our hearts converse,
In shadows' embrace—
our universe.

Moonlit Confessions Extended

To you,
under the moon's gentle light,
I write of love
hidden from sight.
A confession--a secret,
in the night shared,
A testament to a love,
uniquely bared.

By moonlit whispers,
our love is sealed,
In the cover of darkness,
it is revealed.
A silent pact
made under starry skies,
In our moonlit confessions,
our true love lies.

Each word a treasure,
a beacon so bright,
Guiding us through

the darkest night.
In moonlit confessions,
our souls entwine,
In the silent orchestra
of the divine.

The Language of Glances Extended

In glances, a language,
only we know,
A love-note in secret,
letting our feelings show.
Eyes meeting in silence,
a conversation deep,
In our secret language,
promises we keep.

With every look,
a novel written in our eyes,
A tale of love,
under guise.
A language of love—
so pure--so true,
Spoken in glances
between me and you.

In the crowd,
a secret shared with a glance,
In those moments,

our hearts dance.
A silent dialogue,
just for two,
In our eyes,
a love so true.

Veiled in Verse Extended

Veiled in verse,
my love for you sings,
A secret melody,
on silent wings.
Each word a note,
a hidden caress,
A love in shadows,
we silently profess.

In every line,
a hidden message for you,
A declaration of love—
deep and true.
In verses veiled,
our story told,
A love that's brave,
a love that's bold.

Beneath the poetry,
our truth lies,
A love that's written

in the skies.
In veiled verse,
our hearts converse,
In every stanza,
our universe.

The Hidden Garden Extended

In our hidden garden,
love blooms in stealth,
A secret paradise,
our hearts' wealth.
This note, a seed,
in fertile ground laid,
In whispers of love,
our foundation made.

Surrounded by walls,
yet free as the air,
In our hidden garden,
we lay bare.
A sanctuary
where our love can grow,
Away from the world's
prying eyes and woe.

Each flower,
a testament to our love's might,
Blooming in secret,

away from the light.
In our hidden garden,
a world apart,
We nurture the love
that fills our heart.

Echoes in the Dark Extended

Echoes in the dark,
a secret shared,
A love-note to you,
openly declared.
In the quiet of night,
our love finds its voice,
In secrecy,
we make our choice.

With every echo,
our love grows stronger,
In the dark,
we can't hide any longer.
A symphony of whispers,
just for us,
In echoes in the dark--
our love we trust.

Through the silence,
our hearts speak very loud,
In echoes in the dark,

our love unbound.
A secret song
played on the night's stage,
In every echo---
our love, the sage.

Between the Lines Extended

Between the lines
of everyday,
A secret love-note,
I convey.

In mundane moments,
our love finds its way,
A silent ode to you—
every day.

In the quiet moments,
in between,
Our secret love,
unseen but keen.

A whispered promise,
soft and clear,
In between the lines,
our love draws near.

Through the humdrum

of the daily grind,
A secret message,
you will find.

A love that lives
in silent deeds,
In between the lines,
it plants its seeds.

With every word,
a hidden embrace,
Our love finds
its secret place.

Between the lines,
a love so fine,
In every letter,
you are mine.

The Unsung Ballad Extended

An unsung ballad,
for your ears alone,
A secret love,
quietly grown.

This note--a melody,
in your heart played,
In harmonies of love,
our foundation laid.

In silence,
our ballad takes its form,
A love that's weathered
every storm.

An ode to you,
in whispers sung,
An unsung ballad,
from lung to lung.

Through the silence—

our melody soars,
A love that
quietly explores.

In the unsung ballad
of our hearts,
A masterpiece—
where true love starts.

With every beat—
a secret vow,
In our unsung ballad,
we take our bow.

A silent symphony
of two hearts beat,
In our love's melody,
we are complete.

The Hidden Sun Extended

Like the sun,
hidden by the clouds,
Our love—
in secrecy, enshrouds.

This note--a ray of light,
in darkness cast,
A love that shines—
in shadows vast.

Beneath the veil
of the unseen sun,
Our secret love—
second to none.

A warmth that grows,
despite the chill,
In our hidden sun,
love finds its will.

Through the clouds,

our love breaks free,
A hidden sun—
for you and me.

Illuminating
our secret place,
In its warmth—
our love's embrace.

Though hidden now,
our sun will rise,
Above the clouds,
in clearer skies.

Until then--in this note,
my love, I pen,
Our hidden sun,
will shine again.

Shattered Symphony

In our symphony,
the notes turned sour,
As time eroded
our once sweet bower.

Love--once vibrant,
now a faded flower,
Leaves me alone
in the midnight hour.

The melody that once
danced in the air,
Now a haunting refrain
of despair.

Each note a memory,
bitter and bare,
A symphony shattered—
beyond repair.

Our harmony---
lost to the winds of change,
Leaving behind
a love estranged.

In silence,
our hearts now rearrange,
The pieces of a melody—
forever changed.

Yet, in the stillness,
a new tune I compose,
A song of healing,
as my heart foreclose.

From the ruins of us—
a new strength arose,
In shattered symphony,
a new hope glows.

Your goodbye—
a whisper against my skin,
A painful echo—
of what could have been.

In the silence,
your absence cuts deep,
A chasm wide,
where my sorrows seep.

The echoes linger,
a haunting refrain,
A melody of love,
now tinged with pain.

Each memory---
a note in a mournful melody,
Playing on repeat,
a symphony of tragedy.

I reach for you—

but grasp only air,
A phantom presence,
no longer there.

In the quiet,
your echo is my despair,
A constant reminder,
this world is unfair.

Yet, through the pain,
a lesson learned,
In the fire of heartbreak,
my spirit burned.

From the ashes—
a stronger heart emerged,
On the echoes of goodbye—
a new path converged.

Fractured Mirror

In the mirror,
our reflections once danced,
Now, only mine stands,
Fractured and glanced.

Your shadow,
a specter of the past,
A love once bright,
not meant to last.

The shards reflect
a tale of two,
A story of love,
through and through.

But now, the mirror
only shows
A fractured self,
amidst our woes.

I trace the lines

where we did part,
Each crack a testament
to a broken heart.

In the silence,
I stand alone,
A reflection fractured;
a love outgrown.

Yet, in this brokenness,
I find,
A strength to leave
the past behind.

In fractured mirrors,
a new me I see,
Beyond the ruins
of what used to be.

The Last Letter

I penned my heart
in a letter, last,
A testament
to our love, now past.
Words bleeding onto paper,
a final plea,
For the love lost
between you and me.

Each stroke,
a tear that went uncried,
A collection of feelings,
long denied.
The ink runs,
like the love we shared,
Spilling secrets,
once carefully ensnared.

This last letter,
a vessel of my heart's ache,
"Goodbye" to the dreams

we'll never make.
Yet, within these words,
a release I find,
A step towards healing,
leaving pain behind.
Though our story ends
on this sorrowful note,
In this letter, my love,
my final quote:

A goodbye penned
in the depths of the night,
A love remembered,
in the morning light.

Winter's Embrace

Our love, a summer's day,
bright and warm,
Now wrapped in winter's
unforgiving storm.

Your warmth,
a memory fading into the night,
Leaves me yearning
for a lost light.

The chill sets in,
a cold reminder,
Of the heat we shared,
now no finder.

Our summer love,
caught in winter's grasp,
A warmth extinguished,
with a final gasp.

In the frost,

I trace our names,
A reminder of
our extinguished flames.

Yet, with each snowfall,
a cleanse begins,
Washing away the sin—
the pins.

As winter's embrace
tightens its hold,
In its icy grip,
I find my bold.

A heart once warm,
now learning to mend,
Preparing for spring,
when winter's end.

From the ashes
of what we once knew,
I try to find
a single ember of you.

But in the cold,
all that remains
Is the echo
of love's refrains.

Where warmth once lived,
now only chill,
A void that time
refuses to fill.

Our fire, once bright—
reduced to dust,
In the ashes of us,
a broken trust.

Yet, through the gloom,

a lesson learned,
In the fire of loss,
my soul was burned.

But like a phoenix,
from ashes, I rise,
Towards the dawn
of clearer skies.

From the ruins of our love,
a new day begins,
A life rebuilt,
from what was within.

Though our tale ends,
my story goes on,
In the ashes of us,
a new light is drawn.

Unwritten Stars

We plotted our course
by unwritten stars,
Dreams dashed on life's
relentless bars.

Now, alone,
I navigate the dark,
Missing the light
of our extinguished spark.

The map we drew,
now torn and faded,
A journey of hearts,
once elated.

Lost in the cosmos,
our path unclears,
Our starlight dimmed
by each of our tears

But in the night,

a solitary light,
A guide to lead me
from this plight.

The unwritten stars,
a path anew,
A journey within,
born from the rue.

Though our constellations
no longer align,
In the darkness,
I find a sign.

A course charted
by the lessons of heartbreak,
A solitary voyage,
for my own sake.

Hollow Echoes

Our house, once filled
with laughter and light,
Now hollow,
echoes our love's plight.

In every corner,
a memory fades,
In the silence,
our love's cascade.

The echoes of our past,
a haunting tune,
A melody of a love
that ended too soon.

Each step I take,
a reminder of us,
In the quiet,
a heart's mournful fuss.

But in the echoes,
a strength I find,
A resolve,
in the hollows of my mind.

To rebuild,
to laugh, to love anew,
In the echo of
what we once knew.

The silence, once a prison,
now sets me free,
A canvas blank,
for what I'm yet to be.

From hollow echoes,
a new song I compose,
A melody of resilience,
in the face of woes.

The Tides of Farewell

Like the tides,
our love came and went,
A force of nature,
is now spent.

Your absence,
a relentless sea,
Washes what is
left of you from me.

The shore—once ours,
now mine alone,
A landscape of love,
now overgrown.

Each wave--a memory,
crashing in,
A reminder of what
might have been.

But with each tide—

a cleansing comes,
Washing away the pain—
the sums.

A shore reshaped
by the tides of farewell,
A heart healing,
beneath love's spell.

The sea, though harsh,
teaches me to thrive,
In the ebb and flow,
I find my drive.

From the tides of farewell,
I learn to sail,
Onward in waters
once thought frail.

The Curtain Falls

On our stage,
the final act, played,
Love's bright lights,
to darkness, fade.

The curtain falls,
the audience gone,
Leaving me in the shadow,
alone—forlorn.

The applause--once loud,
now a distant dream,
Our love--a play,
lost in the stream.

Each act--a memory,
each scene--a tear,
The final bow—
my greatest fear.

Yet, in the quiet
of the empty hall,
A resolve within,
to stand tall.

The curtain falls,
but the show goes on,
In the theatre of life—
a new dawn.

With every ending,
a beginning anew,
A chance to rewrite—
to review.

Though our play concludes,
my journey persists,
In the aftermath,
my spirit resists.

The Last Dance

We danced in the moonlight,
shadows entwined,
A love so deep,
a bond uniquely designed.

But as the music faded,
so did your grasp,
Leaving me alone,
with a memory to clasp.

The floor now empty,
where once we swayed,
Each step--a memory,
gradually frayed.

In the silence--your absence
a deafening sound,
A heart lost in rhythm,
no longer found.

Yet, in this dance
of love and loss, I learn,
With each turn,
a new strength I earn.

Though our last dance
has come to an end,
In every step,
your love I'll always defend.

Through tears, a smile,
for the love we shared,
A dance of memories,
forever aired.

In the echo
of our last dance, I find,
The courage to leave
our love behind.

When Stars Whisper Goodnight

Under the blanket of night,
where stars align,
I whispered your name,
wishing you were still mine.

The cosmos whispered back—
a lullaby of pain,
A tale of a love lost—
nothing to regain.

Each star--a memory,
burning bright,
In the celestial sea—
a guiding light.

But as dawn breaks,
their brilliance fades,
Just like our love,
into the shades.

Yet, in the whisper of the stars,
a solace I find,
A gentle reminder
of what's left behind.

For even in darkness,
love's light does shine,
In the whispers of stars,
your heart still mines.

The night sky,
a canvas of our love's story,
A testament
to our fleeting glory.

But as stars whisper
"goodnight", I understand,
Love's not in our grasp—
it's in the heart's command.

Echoes of the Heart

The echoes of our laughter,
now halls of silence,
A testament to love's
once radiant brilliance.

Each echo,
a pang of what was lost,
A love so pure,
now covered in frost.

In the stillness,
your voice I yearn to hear,
A sound so sweet,
forever dear.

But in its place,
a void so vast,
A reminder of a love
that couldn't last.

Yet, within these echoes,
a strength I glean,
A power unfound—
unseen,

To rebuild from the ruins
of our love's demise,
Underneath the same
starlit skies.

For though our echoes
may fade into the night,
The love once shared
remains a light.

A beacon through the darkness,
guiding my way,
A reminder that in the heart
love will stay.

Fragments of Us

In the ruins of what
we were--fragments lie,
Scattered pieces of 'us'
under the open sky.
Each shard a story,
a memory--a sigh,
A testament to love
that once flew high.

Amidst the wreckage,
my heart seeks
For a sign--a whisper,
as the soul speaks.
Yet, in the debris,
a beauty I find,
Love's resilience—
undefined.

Though broken,
these fragments of us glow,
Illuminating paths

where new loves grow.
In the ruins,
our story remains a muse,
A reminder that even shattered,
love infuses.

The Final Verse

We wrote our love in verses,
lines entwined,
A poetic journey,
uniquely designed.
But as the final verse
draws near,
I face the ending
with a tear.

The ink runs dry,
the pages bare,
A story ended;
a soul laid bare.
Yet, in this final verse,
a hope does bloom,
Beyond the silence,
beyond the gloom.

For in our verses,
love does live,
A testament to

what we had to give.
And though the final verse
may close our tale,
In the heart of poetry,
love prevails.

In the Quiet Aftermath

In the quiet aftermath
of our storm,
Where silence speaks,
and heartbreaks form.
I find myself wandering,
lost and torn,
In the aftermath of love—
reborn.

The storm that raged,
now a whisper soft,
Leaving behind the scars—
aloft.
Yet, in this quiet,
a strength I find,
A peace of mind—
a redefined.

Through the ruins,
a path I carve,
In the quiet aftermath,

I learn to starve.
For in the silence,
I find my voice,
In the aftermath—
a choice.

Ode to the Unsaid

Words unspoken,
a silent ode,
To the love
that we once code.
In the spaces between,
our story told,
An ode to the unsaid, bold.

The words
we never dared to speak,
Hold the truth
that we seek.
Yet, in their silence,
a power found,
In the unsaid,
we are bound.

An ode to whispers
in the night,
To the love
kept out of sight.

In the silence,
our hearts confide,
In the unsaid—
we reside.

The Price of Dreams

We dreamt in colors—
vibrant and bright,
A palette of love—
in the night.
But dreams,
they come at a cost,
In the pursuit,
something lost.

The price of dreams,
a heartache deep,
A vigil that
we must keep.
Yet, in the cost,
a lesson learned,
In the flames of dreams,
we burned.

But from the ashes,
we rise again,
Stronger--wiser,

through the pain.
For the price of dreams,
while steep,
Is the path where
our souls leap.

The Bridge Between

Between us, a bridge—
once strong and sure,
A connection—
beautifully pure.
But as the days pass,
the bridge did fray,
Leaving us lost—
lost and astray.

The gap widens,
with every word unsaid,
A chasm of regret—
dread.
Yet, in the divide,
a hope does gleam,
For bridges are rebuilt
sometimes only in dreams.

With every step towards
the other side,
In our hearts,

we confide.
For the bridge between,
though fallen apart,
Lives on within the heart.

Our love--a season,
changing--fleeting,
With every heartbeat—
beating.
From the spring of joy,
to summer's heat,
To autumn's fall—
bittersweet.

Winter comes,
with its cold embrace,
A love once warm,
now misplaced.
Yet, in the cycle,
a beauty found,
In every season,
love is crowned.

For seasons change,
and so do we,
In love's seasons,

we are free.
To grow--to learn—
to start anew,
In the seasons of the heart—
true.

Whispers to the Moon

To the moon,
I whisper your name,
A silent prayer--
a flickering flame.

In the night sky,
a connection remains,
With every whisper—
love sustains.

The moon—
a witness to our love's tale,
A beacon in the night—
without fail.

Though apart,
in the moonlight, we meet,
In whispers soft,
in dreams sweet.

For the moon hears
what the heart conceals,
In its glow—
our love reveals.

A whisper to the moon,
carried on the night's breeze,
A bond unbroken,
despite the seas.

Echoes of What Was

In the stillness,
echoes of what was linger,
Memories sharp—
like a splinter.
A love that once
filled the air,
Now echoes in the emptiness—
bare.

Each echo,
a reminder of the past,
Of a love too
bright to last.
Yet, in these echoes,
a melody sweet,
A remembrance of when
two hearts did meet.

Though the music
has faded into silence,
In echoes,

I find a form of solace.
For in the whispers
of what was, I hear,
The love we shared,
forever near.

Stars That Never Align

Like stars in the sky,
we once shined bright,
Two souls in the night,
a spectacular sight.
But as the cosmos decree,
some stars never align,
A celestial fate,
yours and mine.

Our orbits crossed,
a brief encounter,
A moment in time,
a cosmic fount.
Yet, destined
to drift apart,
Leaving behind
a stardust heart.

Though the universe
keeps us afar,
In the night sky,

I find our star.
A reminder of love,
not meant to be,
But in the heavens,
together we're free.

The Art of Letting Go

In the twilight of our love,
a quiet breaking,
A heart once whole,
now slowly aching.

A tapestry of us,
unraveled and worn,
In the art of letting go—
a new self-born.

Our whispers in the night,
now silent screams,
Lost are the dreams
within dreams.

Yet, in this ending,
a grace I find,
The strength to leave
our love behind.

The art of letting go,

a painful muse,
Teaches the heart
to choose.

In every tear,
a lesson learned,
In every goodbye,
freedom earned.

With each step away
from our shared past,
A future bright—
vast.

In the art of letting go,
I discover,
The beauty of life,
to uncover.

The Dawn of My Truth

In shadows long,
I hid my heart,
A silent actor—
playing my part.
But dawn breaks,
and so does my fear,
Into the light,
I step, my path clear.

A journey long,
through nights so deep,
Where tears were sown,
for my soul to keep.
Yet, with each step
towards the rising sun,
I found the courage—
long undone.

For in the light,
my truth shines bright,
A spectrum of colors,

oh, so right.
To myself,
I am finally true,
Embracing the
love I am due.

The Liberation Song

Once caged in fear,
my voice was lost,
A heavy price,
my heart the cost.
But now I sing,
a song so free,
A melody of who
I am meant to be.

This song,
it rises from deep within,
A symphony of where
I have been.
And as I sing, my soul takes flight,
Out of the darkness, into the light.

No longer silent,
my story I share,
A testament of
how much I care.
For every soul

still lost in night,
May my liberation
guide you to the light.

The Reflection I Embrace

In the mirror,
a stranger once stood,
A reflection—
misunderstood.
But now I see,
clear and true,
The person I am—
through and through.

No more hiding—
no more pain,
No longer shall
I live in vain.
For the person
in the mirror now,
Lives life
with a new-found vow.

To be proud,
to love, to embrace,
Each part of me-

every trace.
For in my reflection,
I finally see,
The beauty of being
unapologetically me.

The Rainbow After Rain

After the storm,
the skies were gray,
I wandered lost—
day by day.
But then the rain
began to cease,
And with it came
a sense of peace.

A rainbow arched
across the sky,
A colorful bridge--
way up high.
A sign that though the storm
was dire,
Beyond it lies
a world much brighter.

In that rainbow,
I saw my soul,
A promise that

I could be whole.
For even after
the deepest pain,
There is beauty,
love to gain.

Coming Home

For years, I wandered—
lost and alone,
Searching for a place
to call "home."
A place where love
knows no bounds,
Where my true self
can be easily found.

And though the journey
was long and hard,
Each step left me
visually scarred,
I found that home
was not a place,
But acceptance—
love, and grace.

Home in my heart,
where love resides,
Now in the open,

my true self hides.
Coming out of the shadows,
into the day,
Proudly I stand,
come what may.

The Light Within

In the darkest night,
I found a spark,
A light within,
to dispel the dark.
A flame of hope,
burning bright,
Guiding me through
the longest night.

This light--my beacon—
my guide,
Helped me find
the strength inside.
To step out of the shadows,
and into the sun,
To embrace myself,
the battles won.

For within me
lies a power so great,
To love--to live—

and free to create.
The light within,
now fully shown,
Illuminates the love
I have always known.

The Journey to Me

Through winding paths
and stormy seas,
I searched for someone
I could please.
But the hardest journey,
I came to see,
Was the one that led me
back to me.

A path
of self-discovery,
Of learning to
simply be.
With each step taken—
each hurdle crossed,
I found the parts of me
I thought were lost.

Now at the journey's end,
here I stand,
My heart open--

my soul so grand.
For the greatest love
I came to see,
Was the love I found
deep within me.

Unwritten Chapters

My life--a book,
pages blank,
Filled with moments,
for which I thank.
Each chapter
written in the light,
A story
of my hard fight.

For years,
chapters were dark and cold,
Stories of fear,
I never told.
But now, I write
with a pen so free,
Chapters of love--
of joy--of me.

Unwritten chapters
await ahead,
Filled with hope—

no longer dread.
For in my book,
I now decree,
A life of love—
for the world to see.

The Bridge of Acceptance

I stood before a bridge—
wide and vast,
A path to the future—
away from the past.
This bridge of acceptance,
sturdy and true,
Led to a world where
I could be anew.

Across this bridge,
with each cautious step,
I left behind
the tears I wept.
On the other side,
I found my place,
In a realm of love—
acceptance, and grace.

The bridge behind me,
now a beacon for all,
A reminder that we

can rise after we fall.
To those still standing
on the edge of night,
Cross the bridge
into the light.

Stars of My Own Sky

In the darkness,
I once sought,
Stars in others' skies,
I thought.
But the journey
through the night,
Taught me I have
my own inner light.

Now, I navigate by stars
of my own making,
Constellations of love—
with no faking.
A sky once dark,
now brilliantly aglow,
With lights of self-love—
they now show.

This cosmos within,
so vast and wide,
Is where my

true self resides.
No longer lost in
others' night,
I shine in my own right,
oh, so bright.